The Relationships
of
Above-Average People

5th Printing, 2010

Contents

Relationships and True Purpose

$\mathcal{F}$ew people connect their personal relationships to the true purpose of their lives (i.e., the cosmic purpose of the human soul), but they are connected.

Most relationships fail after all the initial attractions wane because, given time, the subconscious mind of one or both partners evaluates and measures that the other person cannot help them in the search to discover their true purpose. While most people never realize it, this technical process of measurement occurs in almost everyone, as it is a natural function of the sub-conscious mind—and an extension of the grand scheme of nature.

Once the subconscious mind recognizes that the other person cannot help us fulfill our true purpose in life, or, as in many relationships, the other person even holds us back from pursuing our true purpose, only then do we begin consciously to experience all the causes commonly attributed to losing interest in, or falling out of love with, another person. We begin to experience discontent, dissatisfaction, and boredom, or we tire of their ways and habits, or we feel we have evolved and grown while the other person has remained the same.

But long before all these traditional reasons for losing interest in another person are consciously felt, the specific subconscious mind function responsible for guiding us to our true purpose has evaluated that our partner cannot help us fulfill the true purpose of our life, or may in fact be a deterrent. It is only then that we begin to feel that any interest, stimulation, or satisfaction that the other person used to generate has begun to fade.

No matter what a person does, how they look, or whatever their assets, if they are not compatible with our true purpose, the relationship cannot grow. It will end or be ever stagnant and unfulfilling, as many relationships are. This is why we remain unhappy and unfulfilled when we are with the wrong person, and why we are ever-searching and longing for the right person. Whether we realize it or not, what everyone is really looking for is the person who will be a companion and provide comfort while we fulfill the true purpose of our life. For an above-average person, this is the basis that sustains any relationship.

We, then, should never form a relationship or remain in one when the other person is restrictive to the pursuit of our true purpose. Time and our feelings will always clarify who is right for us or who is wrong for us—although above-average people usually know quickly who is not their own kind. Unfortunately, many people, for various reasons, are trapped in their relationships. But ultimately, for above-average people, freedom to pursue their true purpose is their only option. Living without discovering your true purpose is never being fully alive, and you should never allow anyone or anything to stand in your way.

Magic [2]

*E*ach person generates a measurable degree, from negligible to powerful, of charisma—that intangible, cosmic, mysteriously attracting, interesting, stimulating energy that a person radiates to others.

The less of this cosmic energy a partner brings to a relationship, the emptier the relationship. The more each partner brings this cosmic energy to their relationship, the more stimulating and fulfilling that relationship.

People in unfulfilling relationships usually feel an excessive need to seek activities, hobbies, entertainments, and the company of other people outside the relationship to compensate for the emptiness of their relationship. Stimulation of the psyche must be sought elsewhere when the magic that is possible in a relationship is low or nonexistent. People who do not possess enough of their own internal magic usually seek every opportunity to do things and go places as a compensation. The less magic a person possesses, the greater the desire for activities and entertainments, and the grander the scale.

Partners who can generate their own magic experience stimulation and fulfillment from the simplest and most basic activities of life, since their own magic enlivens and excites everything they do. They do not have to depend upon socializing and planned activities to generate interest and stimulation beyond the company of each other. The more the union generates its own magic, the more the partners are content to be in each other's company and usually disdain the burdens of activities and socializing outside the relationship. They are usually relieved to shut out the noisy, troublesome, and commonplace world.

Usually, when one partner generates the magic while the other partner does not, the partner who does, no longer desires or will just tolerate the company of the other partner. Unfortunately, this reality exists in many relationships and is the source of unfulfillment and often of the termination of the relationship. If one partner generates most of the magic and the other feeds on it, the cosmic connection between the partners will die, even if the couple for various reasons remains together.

The secret, of course, to generating cosmic energy, which is charismatic and magical, is to continue to remain open to learning and to change and grow. Egotistical, cosmically immature people who resist constructive criticism and who resist change do not generate the magic of life that is interesting or appealing to above-average people.

People who remain open and continue to evolve, change, and grow generate the most magic, while people who remain basically the same generate the least magic. To experience an ever-renewing, fulfilling relationship, you must be generating your own charisma, and must find a partner who likewise generates their own charisma.

The highly astute person will find that those types of people who continually take classes, buy books, join groups, and adopt methods, techniques, systems, and studies that purport to represent spiritual advancement are the people who usually change the least. Ultimately, it is discovered that these activities and pursuits are, in reality, compensations for those who will not change appreciably their basic nature or motivations in their lifetimes.

Average people are motivated to continually pursue the external labels of change because it is something they will never do. Above-average people simply must desire to change—and a unique process for change will find its way to them. It is the real change of self that always equates to personal magic.

But real magic is not that magical. When you continue to grow and change, you will always have the magic of life at your fingertips—and your relationships will be reflective of your magic.

Potential and Performance

*U*nbeknownst to almost everyone, when we meet someone to whom we are attracted and a relationship begins to develop, our mind, by its natural intuitive capacity, is attracted to that person's potential as much as it is attracted to their actual performance—performance being everything you see in a person's behavior and personality. When we choose someone to date, to live with, or to marry, the human mind instinctively, naturally, and subconsciously measures and experiences the potential in another person's soul and then projects that potential into the relationship.

When anyone is romantically attracted to another person, seldom does that person evaluate a potential partner 100% objectively by their performance, yet above-average people must do just that—distinguish the difference between potential and actual performance.

Subconsciously experiencing a person's potential beyond their actual performance is why people choose unsuitable partners. It is why people stay with other people longer than they should. And it is why the endings of most relationships are so disappointing—because performance seldom equals the potential we subconsciously projected. At the end of a relationship, we finally see the other person 100% objectively—we finally see their performance completely separate from their potential.

It is amazing how few people realize that they are not seeing their partner exactly for who they really are. Rarely does performance equal potential, although we do have to give everyone some allowance to change and to grow, as some people will. But at the same time, we should realize that statistically, most people will not appreciably change their style, their habits, their personalities—their ways—in their lifetime.

But the key for above-average people is always to remain aware of the difference between potential and performance. To decipher correctly the possibilities of any relationship, focus exclusively on the performance of the other person—think performance, and a mechanism of the mind will respond. You will begin to see everyone for who and what they really are, and then you should plan, project, and act accordingly.

Few things waste your life like false hope.

The Biggest Mistake

*I*t should be understood by above-average people that each person is born with the potential to achieve a purpose more significant than all the personal goals they desire in life and wish to accomplish. And their true purpose is, in some way, and to some degree, related to the whole of mankind. The difference between average and above-average people is that the subconscious urge to achieve a higher purpose pulsates in above-average people as much as, or more than, the desire to achieve all personal goals.

In seeking a companion or a mate, the biggest and most commonly made mistake occurs when the subconscious urge stemming from one's true purpose becomes combined with the urge to find a mate. Then, of course, when a relationship develops, it is based on an ill-conceived subconscious emotional foundation. The desire to fulfill a true purpose has erroneously been added to the desire to find a companion, making the need for a companion feel much greater than it actually is, or should be.

This excessive need or desire for a relationship creates a value and dependency on the relationship far beyond what it actually represents by cosmic standards—meaning the importance of the relationship as a means to fulfillment feels much greater than it actually is.

It is this mistake that causes the high degree of discomfort and emotional pain that often occurs with the break-up of a relationship or a marriage. The mistake was: the subconscious emotional investment in the relationship was far greater than it should have been because the subconscious mind became misprogrammed. The loss of the person was not just the loss of a companion, but now also erroneously represents the loss of fulfilling one's true purpose, even though these are two completely different aspects of life.

The above-average mentality should remain aware that the degree of energy and desire to find a companion must be limited to the relevance of a companion in one's life—i.e., companionship, family, love, etc. And the search for one's true purpose, which is the highest reason for life and the means to true fulfillment, requires an energy and desire equal to its relevance.

But erroneously seeking or desiring a mate by using any of the subconscious desire that belongs to seeking and desiring one's true purpose will form a subconscious emotional dependency on another person far greater than it should be and will become the subconscious set-up for emotional devastation or a long period of emotional pain if the relationship ends. This is why, for many people, the breakup of a relationship is so emotionally debilitating and painful. We are erroneously and subconsciously experiencing the loss of our true purpose, which is the highest goal of life, when in reality, we are only losing a companion, and no matter how valuable we feel they are, they are still a lesser goal of life than one's true purpose.

The key, then, for emotional protection for above-average people is to remain mindful at the beginning of every relationship that a partner is only another person, *not* your true purpose in life. Never attribute to any relationship more than its value—i.e., compared to the true purpose for your life. Do not mistakenly desire and value a relationship with any of the energy that belongs to the search for your true purpose. *Never replace purpose with a person.* And by seeking your true purpose above all else, your emotional balance with *all* relationships will maintain the appropriate perspective in the subconscious mind. Then, if a relationship ends, the emotional impact will be relative to the actual loss and will be far less in degree and length of time. If a relationship ends, you are only losing a person, you are not losing the purpose of your life.

Of course, if you are the one who desires to end the relationship, the emotional impact is usually less for you than for your partner. But almost everyone experiences at least one or more major heartbreaks in their lifetime. For above-average people, placing the value of pursuing one's true purpose above a relationship is the correct course in life and is emotional insurance that's wise to have.

Predictable, Mechanical People

*A*nimals function completely by instinct; humans are both creative and operate by instinct—as instinct is nature's mechanism for survival.

Some people, however, because of their upbringing, environmental influences, and their own innate natures, function much more than others by instinct, habit, and a mechanical personality. Habitual, mechanical, predictable behavior in people is, over time, generally not appealing, and becomes destructive to a relationship. Sensitivity, spontaneity, and creativity of personality are usually attractive and almost always give life to a relationship.

Instinct is a good quality when it is used to make practical decisions and to navigate through life. But living too much by instinct and subconscious habit patterns becomes mechanical, predictable, and inconsistent with inspiration, spontaneity, and sensitivity—the qualities that usually sustain a relationship.

Sensitive, spontaneous people should never form serious relationships with habitual, mechanical people. And yet, creative, sensitive people are often attracted to excessively instinctive, habitual people because in the beginning of a relationship, mechanical people seem strong, worldly, dedicated, professionally poised and skilled. They are often successful—and sometimes they have nice faces and bodies. But over time, the sensitivity and spontaneity of one partner will contrast with the habitual and mechanical behavior of the other, and disenchantment almost always sets in and deepens over time. Whoever said opposites attract was right, but neglected to add that they don't necessarily make each other happy.

Sensitive, spontaneous, cosmically aware people are naturally attuned and responsive to the energy and flow of the moment, while habitual, mechanical people are relatively insensitive to the flow and dictates of the moment and operate more by a fixed style, making predictable choices generated by their own habitual thought process. These people wear very thin over time.

It's best that cosmically aware people do not form serious relationships with mechanical, predictable people, because it is the breeding ground for unhappiness, unless the mechanical partner can change to become more sensitive, spontaneous, and responsive to the dictates and flow of the moment. But for those hoping for a change in a mechanical type person—good luck. Those types seldom can change or seldom even want to change.

In life, it's always best to seek your own kind. With a cosmic mate, you have the best chance of achieving satisfaction and fulfillment in a relationship.

Disagreements

You never work out disagreements; you always work them in.

The status of any relationship is always the mathematical sum total of every disagreement you ever had with your partner—and when relationships end, it is the sum total of all the disagreements that caused the break.

Contrary to common belief, emotional disagreements are never resolved. They get permanently recorded in a person's subconscious mind and accumulate as part of a person's subconscious record. The common mistake that most people make is believing that disagreements go away because they go away from the conscious mind. But nothing ever disappears from the subconscious mind. Every exchange and every event, no matter how minute, is recorded, permanently filed, and compounded in the subconscious mind—

and every decision a person makes is the result of their entire subconscious record.

Continually resolving or weathering the same disagreements does not improve a relationship. An episode of emotional discord with a partner may fade from the conscious mind as a person gets busy again with the activities and responsibilities of life, but the discord never fades in the subconscious mind. Continual emotional discord destroys a relationship by degrees. When relationships end, it is because the last straw has been placed on the camel's back. Relationships can only grow and last when people change over time in ways that reduce the cause of the disagreements—not when we give up, and accept our partner's ways, because we realize they will never change.

Learning to live with or tolerate other people's "ways" that they should change is not a resolution or an improvement of a relationship; it's just con- trolled unhappiness, which determines the status of a relationship—and which some people are willing to live with or, for various reasons, are trapped in. However, we all know that just because two people are still together does not mean that the essence of their relationship has not died.

But the question is always the same—have you found the right partner? And the answer is always the same—detect as early as possible a person's ability and willingness to change. For above-average people, sameness in a relationship (i.e., being with a person who doesn't change) becomes restrictive, insufferable, and cosmically claustrophobic.

The unwillingness of a partner to change is a fatal disease for most relationships. If disagreements with a partner continue to arise and the causes are the same, then one way or another the relationship is most likely doomed. If a person's willingness to change has a pulse, the relationship has a chance. Above-average people should never consider a future with anyone who won't change. An above-average person can only flourish in an atmosphere of change; otherwise the pursuit of your own potential will be restricted.

Draining or Feeding Relationships

*T*he more you need a relationship, the less you bring to it. The less you need a relationship, the more you bring to it. The more a person needs or depends on another person for emotional stability and fulfillment, the more they become a continuous, subconscious drain—even though they don't mean to, want to, or in most cases, don't even realize they are doing it.

No one partner is ever completely free of emotionally taxing the other; however, in most relationships, one partner usually drains the other to a much greater degree. And while the person being emotionally drained the most certainly feels it consciously, eventually most of the emotional drain is registered and recorded in the subconscious mind below conscious awareness.

In longstanding relationships, the emotional drain becomes less conscious and recedes more and more to the subconscious level and then is tolerated by a partner, if the drainer delivers enough other contributions to the relationship to offset the drain. In this, everyone's tolerance of an emotional weight varies. In time, the ratio of emotional give and take becomes fixed between boundaries and becomes the standard of the relationship and determines its status. If, however, the subconscious, emotional weight of one partner continues to grow heavier over time until the quality of life becomes insufferable for the other, affection will die and the relationship will usually come to an end.

People who are emotionally self-sufficient, independent-minded, comfortable with and by themselves, and who can extract the benefits that exist in every circumstance and environment are the people who usually do not subconsciously drain other people, and who usually feed their relationships.

People who are cosmically unfulfilled, void of a meaningful purpose, low in sensitivity, overly possessive, controlling, and egotistical, are people who register negatively in the subconscious minds of others—and create a sub-conscious drain.

While we all consciously experience the effects our partners have on us, the subconscious mind registers with mathematical precision the effect when they enter our environment, i.e., either the addition of an emotional weight, or a sense of freedom and relief from the collective stress of life.

People who are, for the most part, uncompromising, dominating, in-sensitive to the dictates of the moment, too much the product of their up-bringing, and who require too much management to create a comfortable atmosphere, usually trigger a subconscious sense of negative weight when they enter our environment. When these people are our partners, they restrict the growth of a relationship over time, limiting its potential—which causes a perpetual discontent within the relationship. These are the drainers.

People who are relatively secure within themselves, positive in their approach to life, unselfish, innately empathetic, sensitive, and cosmically aware usually give us a subconscious sense of relief and freedom when they enter our environment. When these people are our partners, they expand the dimension of the relationship, giving it room to grow into new creative territory and keeping the relationship ever fresh and renewed. These are the people who feed a relationship.

In long-term relationships, except for egregious deficiencies that cause constant conflicts, the effect that each partner has on the other eventually becomes almost completely subliminal. Regardless of what a person may say about their relationship, or even what they may think to themselves at any given time, most people continually equivocate when assessing the status of their relationship and their true feelings for their partner—except when a relationship has clearly died.

Ultimately, the status of every relationship will depend upon whether you are with someone who is a subconscious emotional weight and continuously drains you, or you are with someone who subconsciously generates a degree of relief and freedom from life's burdens whenever you are with them.

The test that you have found the right person is that your partner instinctively allows you the necessary amount of time, space, and emotional freedom to pursue your true purpose—they are always there when you need them, but never become an emotional weight, which is a constant distraction from the pursuit of your true purpose.

If your partner does not subconsciously lift your spirits to some degree every time they enter your environment, you are with the wrong person. Lost time with the wrong person is something you cannot reclaim. So choose your partner wisely, and allow no one to limit the potential of your life.

Marriage

*A*s hard as it may be to believe, and as many people as there are who may disagree, the truth is that most people get married because they run out of options—and getting married is just the next thing to do on the List of Life. Most people are subconsciously and historically programmed to get married as an eventuality and an inevitability.

In actuality, no relationship stands still. Every relationship, at some level, is either growing and developing, or declining. The human mind is subconsciously programmed for progress in all areas of life, including relationships. When any relationship stagnates, one or both partners become dissatisfied, and the relationship begins to decline.

While every human being is unique, and thus all relationships are unique, every relationship, from its inception, must run its course, until there are the inevitable choices: get married, separate, or live together permanently, which more and more people are doing—but they are still a minority of the population. Usually, one partner gets restless and wants to symbolically make the relationship official, i.e., get married.

There are many reasons why people feel the urge to get married—most because they are traditionally programmed, some because of practical or religious reasons, some who need a sense of permanency, and more people than we realize who are pressured into marriage by their partners. But as stated, while some or all of these reasons can accompany the decision to marry, the overriding reason for most marriages is that the partners have run out of options—and the relationship reaches the pressure point of "marry or move on."

Yet, approximately 50% of all marriages end in divorce, another 25% of married couples are unhappy and unfulfilled in their marriage, and nearly all the rest who are not necessarily unhappy or unfulfilled are leading relatively traditional, ordinary, mundane existences, i.e., careers, family, home improvements, travel and leisure, hobbies, socializing, general busyness, and hopefully doing some good deeds—all of which do not seem ordinary or mundane to them, and which suit them just fine. But in the true sense of the term "blissful marriages," there are very few.

One would think that given the number of people who have gotten married since the institution began thousands of years ago, the formula for a blissful marriage would have been found. That formula is: that each partner should be capable of supporting, assisting, and cooperating with the other in the pursuit of their true purpose in life. That means the partners must possess nearly equal sensitivity and cosmic awareness. This is a rare occurrence, and it is why a truly successful marriage is rare.

True fulfillment can only be experienced in any human being by discovering and executing one's true purpose. If your partner is not helping you in the pursuit of your true purpose, they may be, in effect, a hindrance to that goal. Then, as statistically predictable, the marriage will end, or become an unhappy, unfulfilled arrangement, or a traditional and mundane existence, which is acceptable to many average people but which is seldom acceptable, and is often even abhorrent, to the above-average person.

For above-average people, a marriage can only work if you intuitively know your partner will be a helpmate in your search to fulfill the true purpose for your life. A blissful marriage is not two people living out their lives together in Ordinaryville, but two people who are helping each other continually progress toward fulfilling the true purpose for their lives. For above-average people, it is the only formula that is acceptable.

The Lifespan of a Relationship

$\mathcal{A}$ great historical misconception exists about relationships: an almost automatic, subconscious assumption and expectation of permanency. This misconception usually results in disappointment of one or both partners when a relationship comes to an end.

But in reality, from the cosmic perspective, that is, the perspective of nature, every relationship has its own natural lifespan based on many factors, the prime ones being differences in soul content, differences in subconscious record and true purpose, and the differences in each partner's rate of growth. And as unbelievable as it may sound, the lifespans of many relationships are relatively determined on the day they begin.

Just as one person's lifespan may be 90 years, another 50, another 75, and another 36, relationships, too, have their own lifespans. And just as there are many factors, like sickness and accidents, which can shorten a natural lifespan, and other factors which can lengthen the lifespan of a person, so too, there are many factors which can shorten or lengthen the natural lifespan of a relationship. But again, considering all the discord, anger, disappointment, hurt, and the myriad causes and details that usually accompany the end of a relationship, it's hard to believe that almost all relationships actually *do* end at their natural termination point, i.e., as much from a process of nature as from personal discontent and discord between partners.

While this information does little, for some, to reduce the pain and disappointment experienced at the end of a relationship, the person with above-average mentality should consider that when a relationship ends, while it may have many unpleasant, hurtful, and disruptive factors, it is also ending for a cosmic reason. The relationship has run its natural course and can't produce any more than it already has in terms of better positioning one or both partners toward the pursuit of their true purpose in life. The natures of each partner, the subconscious habit patterns of each, the differences in the subconscious urge to fulfill a more meaningful purpose, the ability or lack of ability to change, and the desire or lack of desire to change in one partner, or both, will eventually create a distance that makes the partners incompatible.

The above-average person, experiencing the termination of a relationship, must realize that it is a precise law of the Creation that nothing ends without a mathematically comparable beginning of something new. In cosmic science, which governs existence, all that ends, without exception, does so to allow for a new beginning.

No matter how high the degree of emotional discomfort experienced due to the end of a relationship, as much focus as possible should be placed on what is going to replace what is ending. It is true, the ending of a relationship is very vivid, tangible, well-referenced in the subconscious mind, and usually emotionally charged, and what is to begin is as yet intangible, unknown, and has no specific references to offer comfort. And yet a person must keep looking for the subtle clues, hints, guidance, and direction that are hidden in everything and everyone in their environment. Almost everyone you meet has information for you, even if, most of the time, they do not realize they are delivering it. The key is, the more you remain open to the subtle clues to your future that are always within your immediate environment, the more you will be able to see and hear them. By constantly watching and remaining open, an innate mechanism of mind will become sensitized, and more and more, the unique information for you will become apparent. The keys to your future are ubiquitous. It is a facet of nature that wherever you are, the clues will be there.

In this, one does not need to have faith, but only to understand this law of cosmic science: that whatever is ending is always making room for a mathematically corresponding beginning of something new. And what will come will ultimately better suit one's true future and one's true purpose—and if you remain open, the guidance to your future will always be available. These are nature's immutable laws that you can always trust.

Finding the Right Person

The way to find the right person is to stop looking.

Truly, too high a desire to find the right person, which most people have, is actually the main deterrent to finding the right person. Excessive desire to find the right person ill positions the subconscious mind, which causes a person inadvertently to keep making the wrong decisions and the wrong choices in pursuit of the right person.

Ironically, when you stop looking, only then is the subconscious mind correctly positioned to find the right person, i.e., only then is the intuitive guidance system to find the right person, which is innate to all human beings, accurate.

The reality is: the harder you search for the right person, the less chance you have of finding that person, and the more likely you will keep connecting with the wrong people, because excessive desire always obscures intuitive guidance and sensitivity. The proof is in the fact that most of the time when people believe they have found the right person, they are disappointed afterwards.

But the right person for each of us actually does exist. This reality is consistent with the mathematical balance of nature because the compatibility of a certain person for each of us is relevant to the assistance we need to find and execute our true purpose—which is the purpose for life itself.

The secret, then, of finding the right person, is to redirect the energy, desire, and effort in looking for the right person to instead searching for your true purpose; then, indirectly, you will be led to the right person for you. By making your main focus in life discovering your true purpose, you in effect become a cosmic magnet to attract the right person—because, from the standpoint of nature, the most compatible and fulfilling person for you is the person who is also connected to you through your true purpose. Everyone else, no matter how attractive or promising, will eventually turn out to be disappointing and unfulfilling.

It's natural, to a moderate degree, to always be searching for your true partner. But, if you make the common, age-old mistake of trying to satisfy the ache of unfulfillment with a relationship instead of your true purpose, that will practically guarantee you will never find the right person. Only by seeking your true purpose above all else, do you cosmically set in motion the forces of nature that will attract the person who will help you, support you, and love you in your search for the true reason for your life.

Just as everything in Nature is in perfect mathematical balance with everything else, by the same principle, everyone possesses an innate guidance system to find the partner who will help them achieve their true purpose. The same law that maintains the balance of all of nature applies to human beings as well.

Unfortunately, for most people, their subconscious record of their upbringing and conditioning, i.e., their conditioned preferences, often distorts the innate guidance system that leads them to the right person. But by pursuing your true purpose as the main focus of your life, the inner mind becomes better positioned to lead you to the right person and to attract the right person to you. In this, you can always trust the mechanics and balance of Nature.

Between Relationships: Aloneness and Growth

*F*or above-average people, the times of greatest personal growth in their lives come between relationships—when they are alone, when they feel lonely for a compatible companion, and especially during the times when the ache of loneliness is the strongest.

Loneliness is a form of emotional pain. Evolved people know that emotional pain can be exchanged for spiritual currency, and spiritual currency buys growth, awareness, and greater sensitivity. While the ache of loneliness is an uncomfortable feeling, it is one of the most fertile, positive psychological positions for human growth.

Few people realize how much a relationship engages and consumes the subconscious mind. Approximately 90% of a relationship engages the subconscious mind, while only 10% comprises the actual, physical aspects of a relationship. The more involved you are in a relationship, the more your subconscious mind reacts to the activities, events, adjustments, considerations, and concerns to accommodate the relationship. Subconsciously you carry the full weight of a relationship even when you are not with the other person, or are not even specifically thinking about them.

Human growth depends on the degree to which the subconscious mind of a person receives the contents of their soul. The more a person's subconscious mind is consumed by the totality of a relationship, the less receptive it is to the subtle guidance and direction from the soul.

While loneliness, especially extreme loneliness, feels unpleasant, the absence of another person is always the most fertile condition for soul infusion into the subconscious mind. And the greater the ache of loneliness, the better the conditions for soul infusion and growth.

The more there are activities and busyness in a person's life, especially with the involvement of an emotionally charged relationship, the more the subconscious mind reacts to the physical, surface events of one's environment. The less activity there is in a person's life, the more the subconscious mind reaches inward toward the soul to extract its contents.

Many average people who, because of their nature, receive less soul content, purposely cultivate very busy lifestyles to compensate for their lack of cosmic growth—although they themselves do not understand their motivation to stay excessively busy. Usually, the busier people are, the more they are disconnected from their own soul and the more they rely on physicality to compensate. But even for above-average people, during unavoidable times of excessive busyness, the connection between the subconscious mind and the soul is less active.

Being excessively consumed by any relationship, especially new relationships where emotional content is very high, or an ongoing relationship that remains troubled or unfulfilled, engages the human psyche to such a high degree that a person cannot hear or feel the inner voice of soul guidance.

Few people like to live their lives without a compatible partner, but for many people, the major growth period of their lives comes when they are on their own—between relationships.

If you are an above-average person, you should understand that when you feel lonely, the loneliness is always working for you, and the lonelier you feel, the closer the subconscious mind draws to the soul to extract its contents. Then, when you do form a new relationship, you bring something to it that you didn't have before, because you yourself are someone new whom you were not before.

Affairs, Liaisons, Attractions, Passions, and Loyalty

*W*hen we are physically attracted to another person, there is always, of course, intrigue, adventure, excitement, sexual desire and, when we are romantically accepted by that other person, an ego high.

It's true that these human desires and experiences exist exclusively on their own terms, but these very common experiences and feelings are not always what they appear to be.

Souls recognize other souls; souls maintain eternal soul records; souls communicate with each other and stimulate each other; and some of what human beings feel from and about other human beings is soul-sourced.

It's true that soul recognition, communication, and stimulation between people often translates into emotional adventures, passions, affairs, and ego elevation, but at the level of the soul, where physicality does not exist, the connection between people relates to soul business. And soul business always concerns the reason for a person's life, i.e., the unique higher purpose beyond a successful career, an adequate relationship, family, material expansion, hobbies, entertainment, and even beyond an adequate number of good deeds. Souls will recognize in each other, from soul records, something from the past, a potential for the present, or the possibility of a result in the future—which relates to each person's higher purpose.

The magnetism, desire, or emotional "pressure" to connect with another person may be mostly physical attraction, which is sourced in the subconscious mind, or it may be a soul attraction, sourced in the soul and relating ultimately to each person's purpose in life but accompanied by, or misinterpreted as only a romantic, sensual attraction. It is always difficult to determine the primary source of the magnetism between two people, because while it can be caused by two different sources (the subconscious mind or the soul) there is only one emotional center in the mind that registers the stimulation and excitement of a connection with another person.

Average people are more likely to be attracted to each other mostly from the subconscious level, which results in ordinary relationships and the traditional activities of life. Above-average people are more likely to be attracted to each other at the soul level, which does not preclude a sensual, romantic attraction as well.

Souls transcend lifetimes, souls transcend subconscious records of a current lifetime, and souls transcend the conventional needs and desires of people. But souls have unfinished business with each other from past lifetimes, souls have current business with each other, and souls have potential future business with each other.

Although the motivations for many relationships are obvious, and the results predictable, we should, as policy, never presume to judge why people are attracted to each other, or whether, in our opinion, they are suitable for each other, or judge when people have short or long-term extra-marital relationships, or leave people for other people, or any of the other myriad possible variations of human relationships.

While the world is full of scoundrels and scoundrelettes, it is also filled with sensitive, above-average people who unavoidably have cosmic attractions to each other and even cosmic business, and who feel compelled to explore, experiment, experience, go forward, and accept the consequences, whatever they may be.

Sometimes it's a cosmic thing.

How and Why Relationships Die

*A*lmost all long-term relationships die because of the different rates of growth of the partners.

Growth, as it applies to man, is consistent with the laws of all of nature. Human growth is factored into the mechanics and mathematics of the Creation, and beyond all its personal relevance, on the grander scale, human growth relates to the evolution of mankind.

But the factor of free will, which all human beings are given, can become a hindrance to the natural growth process. Misuse of free will creates habits, and certain habits are blocks to the natural growth process.

While subconscious habit patterns are among the strongest hindrances to growth, there are also other factors that contribute positively or negatively to human growth—the subconscious record of upbringing, intellectual capacity, degree of sensitivity, and the innate nature of a person.

Average people grow moderately in their lifetimes, and just change and mature naturally with time and from circumstances. Many people hardly grow at all after they reach adulthood, but just continue to become older and more experienced versions of their same self. Above-average people, who possess a higher level of sensitivity and an innate sense of true purpose, tend to grow the most in their lifetimes, and tend to grow toward their innate potential.

Different people, because of their different natures, different sub-conscious records, different levels of sensitivity, and different degrees of desire to find the true purpose for their lives, have different degrees of connection between their souls and their subconscious minds—because it is the subconscious mind that facilitates access to the soul.

The more a person is capable of receiving the contents of their own soul, the greater is the potential for a person's growth. The less a person is capable of receiving soul content into their subconscious mind, the less potential there is for growth in that person's nature. Technically, this is why one partner, over time, outgrows the other. People who access the contents of their soul are interesting, stimulating, intriguing, charmingly mysterious, inspiring, and spiritually sensual. People who do not access the contents of their own soul live without a true purpose, project sameness, are shallow and predictable, are usually self-focused and depend on materialism to give life meaning and, to above-average people, quickly lose appeal. The degree of soul content a person receives into their subconscious mind ultimately determines a person's "vibration" and ultimately defines their personality and whether they continue to grow or not. And with a difference in growth between partners comes differences in perspectives on life, differences in lifestyle choices and goals for the future, differences in feelings of one for the other, and differences in the desire to remain together. A difference in the rate of growth between partners is the main reason love dies.

It is usually the partner who outgrows the other who wishes to end the relationship first and wishes to find another person and a lifestyle equal to the level they have attained. Sometimes the partner who has been outgrown senses the hopelessness because of the distance between themselves and their partner and initiates the ending. Either way, as we outgrow a partner, we proportionately lose feeling for them and, often, they for us.

While the growth of one partner beyond the other is the reason for the demise of most relationships, it is also the birth of a new level of life for the person who is willing to pay the price for growth.

Permanency

*I*f you truly believe you have found the person you would choose to spend the rest of your life with, or when you do find that person, then mastering the "who's-at-fault" syndrome is of primary importance.

Couples periodically, often inexplicably, begin to pull away from each other, i.e., from the customary degree of closeness and familiarity they normally share. But who actually triggers this distancing process? Each partner is almost always positive it was the other—as one partner suddenly appears to be in a bad mood, or an odd mood, or seems unaccountably distant, less communicative, abrupt, or irritated, or radiates a negative vibration or uses a body language that is obviously different, creating an uncomfortable atmosphere.

Couples who have been together for a while pick up very quickly and unmistakably when their partner has entered negative territory. Then the negativity of one partner usually triggers the negativity of the other. A process begins of an action and a counter-action, sometimes subtle and unspoken, sometimes more obvious in tone and manner. A distance is created and increases and deepens with time. This is the "who's-at-fault" syndrome. Each partner is sure the fault lies with the other or has been started by the other, and each one reacts more and more to the deteriorating atmosphere.

Among average people, this is a common occurrence, and part of the ups and downs of all relationships — almost a natural way of life. It is, however, the frequency and intensity of the distancing process that ultimately determines the status of any relationship, since the collective negativity becomes part of the permanent subconscious record of each partner's reference of the other.

The more frequent and intense these episodes of distancing occur, the less a relationship will grow. The less frequent these episodes, the more a relationship will strengthen and reach new experiential and creative territory between the partners.

It is important to understand that every time an episode of distancing occurs, the relationship regresses to a lower level—then when the episode ends, the couple must reestablish the level that existed before, hence, the ups and downs of most relationships which continually retrace the same emotional and experiential territory until a range is eventually established within which the couple usually operates for the entire lifespan of the relationship. It is difficult for a relationship to grow when the partners must repeatedly return to a previous level instead of reaching new territory. It is why many people are motivated to seek outside interests, entertainments, and the company of others in order to compensate for a relationship that exists between fixed boundaries and does not grow.

But above-average people can expect more from their relationships and more from life. Above-average people have the potential with the same partner to continually reach new experiential and creative territory—making the relationship ever new, always surprising, and fulfilling.

The secret, then, is: as soon as it becomes apparent to either or both partners that the distancing process has begun, *stop it*. The specific issue of the moment is insignificant compared to the larger issue—*growth*. In the grand scheme of each partner helping the other to achieve their true purpose, it doesn't matter who started the distancing process. Stopping the negative spiral, which is counterproductive to cosmic progress, is what is vital.

Even if one wanted to ascribe blame as to who started the negativity, it is almost impossible because it's always an ultra-subtlety from one partner that strikes a negative subconscious chord in the other, who then in turn reacts with a negative response, and so on and so on. Even the original subtlety from one partner could have been triggered by an equally subtle action of the other partner. Like the chicken and egg—one never knows which came first.

But in the pursuit of permanency, both partners must be of the intellectual caliber to realize the importance of focusing on the potential damage of the process, above the issue of the moment. Both partners must cooperate to stop the negative process. The partner who recognizes the spiral first must take the initiative to address the subject. Both partners must cooperate by talking it through—with the goal being to stop the spiraling process. What the issue is, and who is right or wrong, is always of lesser importance. Stopping the process quickly is the main focus and the means for growth—even if it takes something as radical as seeing and feeling the other person's point. The sooner a partner feels the distancing begin and addresses it, the easier it is to stop; the longer the process continues, the harder it is to return to positive territory. The instinct of most people is to react and retaliate. The instinct of an above-average person is to stop the distancing as soon as possible.

Recognizing the distancing process as early as possible, and using the psychological skill to stop it, will yield benefits and experiences for the relationship that most other people don't even know exist. And if the partners are right for each other, it practically ensures permanency.

Love Is a Business

*W*hen people decide to marry, live together, or date each other exclusively, we assume they are in love with each other. Rarely, however, do any two people love each other to the exact same degree or in the same way. Almost always, the love of one partner is, to some degree, more or less than the love of the other. The human capacity for love is a very complex subject and varies uniquely with each person.

However, more than most people realize, love is a business and the human subconscious mind is its very accurate accountant. In its ultimate definition, love is sacrifice and the degree of love is usually consistent with the degree of sacrifice one partner makes for the other. While there are many forms of sacrificing, it is only when the sacrifice is relatively equal that love can flourish. The closer to a 50/50 give-and-take ratio between two people, the better the climate for love to be sustained and grow.

But there are many ways people can give to each other and take from each other—materially, financially, sexually, psychologically, emotionally—and the give-and-take process within all the categories is extremely intricate and unique to every couple. Yet there is a part of the subconscious mind that is always objectively keeping an accurate record, and in that sense, love is a business. When one partner takes more than they give or gives more than they take for too long a time, then the business of love begins to go bad.

As we view the relationships of others, one partner may appear to be giving much more to the other, or one may appear to be taking much more from the other. And at times, the give-and-take ratio you see between people on the surface may be accurate. But the give-and-take process involves both tangibles and intangibles. One partner may be giving more tangibles to the other but may be receiving an equal number of intangibles, such as a degree of emotional stability, companionship in any of its myriad forms, or even a form of subconscious security resulting from familiarity.

Tangibles include any form of observable, physical behavior of one partner toward the other, while intangibles include the subconscious effects that one partner has on another. All tangible behavior and intangible effects can be either positive or negative. If the tangibles from one partner appear somewhat negative, but the intangibles that person provides are relatively positive, there would be an adequate balance in the relationship, even if it appears to an observer to be imbalanced.

Almost always, the give-and-take process between couples exists in inexplicable forms and a labyrinth of subconscious subtleties, and is unique with every couple. But, regardless of the form, the subconscious mind never stops tabulating the percentages of what a person is giving and what a person is receiving. Ultimately, as unromantic as it may seem, at the subconscious level, love becomes a business. If one partner incurs too high a debt and not enough credit, like any business, the relationship will fail.

Unfortunately, most people are relatively unaware of the precise give-and-take ratio of their relationships since it occurs at so many different levels and requires an extraordinary sensitivity to measure. However, this is a subject that above-average people must examine and accurately measure.

The above-average person can appreciate that, beyond all the more traditionally recognized personal aspects of a relationship, additionally love is a business. So, if you have found the person you wish to build a lasting relationship with, then it should be run like a business. Make sure you give your partner a good product at a reasonable price, and always be sensitive to the math: *give as much as you take*.

Soul Mates

*M*ost people still believe the myth that another person can be their soul mate. It is very common for people to misinterpret the inner drive, ache, and longing to claim their own soul content as the desire to find some unknown perfect companion. After all, most people live their entire lives and never realize that accessing the contents of their own soul is the most important goal of life, while seeking a suitable mate is one of the most common instincts and pursuits. Many people believe the ache of unfulfillment and the need for completion can be satisfied by finding the right person. But, completion is the responsibility of the self with the self, and unfortunately, many people will forever be seeking and expecting another person to do for them what they must do for themselves.

The degree of fulfillment that everyone is subconsciously seeking can only result from finding one's true purpose—not by finding another person. The proof is: even when one does find the right person, if their true purpose is not discovered, the ache of unfulfillment will always return.

Above-average people should understand that your soul mate is not another person—your soul mate is the contents of your own soul. When you adjust your consciousness (i.e., prepare your mind) to receive the contents of your soul, the mating takes place between your conscious mind and the contents of your soul—then you become aware of your true purpose, and the ways and means to achieve it.

The right person for us can provide us with companionship, friendship, love, intimacy, support, and encouragement in the pursuit of our true goal, but they themselves are never the true goal. The person with an average mentality commonly mistakes the base of life, i.e., a companion, family, career, and financial security, as the goal of life itself, when these factors are only a base of comfort from which to launch to discover the true purpose. The strong desire to find a soul mate, in reality, is often the need to compensate for the inability to connect with the contents of one's own soul. It is typical cosmic ignorance to mistake the urging of the soul to find one's purpose for the urge to find a companion.

While above-average people, like everyone else, need companionship, intimacy, love, and friendship, they learn not to rely on another person to complete their lives. In the pursuit of one's true purpose, no one should allow themselves to become vulnerable to another person or to be held emotionally hostage by the decisions of another person.

Scientifically considering the full capacity of the human mind, one should understand that only 10% or less of its capacity can give to any relationship 100% of all the relationship requires and needs to completely satisfy and fulfill it—leaving 90% or more for the necessities of life and the pursuit and execution of one's true purpose—and this is as it should be. Then, if a relationship must end, only 10% of the emotional center of the mind is vulnerable to emotional damage. It is difficult for many people to comprehend that you can fully love another person and fully satisfy a relationship and yet remain, for the most part, detached in the pursuit of your true purpose. There is no reason to limit the capacity of the human mind.

Your true purpose, then, is your soul mate, not another person. Your true purpose will never lie to you, never cheat you, never deceive you, and never leave you. Your true purpose is never in a bad mood, and never gets angry at you; your true purpose remains ever and completely loyal to you. Your true purpose has a voice, and whenever you speak to it, it will answer you—and if you seek it above all else, the answers will always be correct. Ultimately, it is the source of your happiness, your fulfillment, and your power. And while all else in life may waver, disappoint, or end, your true purpose is always your best friend for life, as it is based in your soul.

While your true purpose is your soul mate, the right person is the mate of your true purpose. While the feelings are similar, above-average people learn not to confuse the desire to find the right person with the impulse to find their true purpose, and they instinctively know which is always the higher priority.

Soul Compatibility

Remember the title of this book, "The Relationships of Above-Average People." That means, of course, that the material relates to a specific group of people who are interested in and capable of achieving a goal that people of lesser mentalities may not be.

To above-average people, the existence, mechanics, contents, and purpose of the soul are equally as relevant, or more relevant, than all other aspects of life. To average people, the more easily discernible and gratifying material aspects of life are usually more desired and pursued.

When an above-average person meets another above-average person and they are attracted to each other, there is soul recognition, soul engagement, the potential for soul compatibility and soul purpose. But a relationship, once formed, will level off, stagnate, and deteriorate if soul compatibility is not achieved, because once the "giddiness" of newness wears off, the partners will experience varying degrees of limitation and frustration in the relationship. They will continually feel there is something missing—something more to experience and achieve from the relationship that is never forthcoming. This feeling, strong enough and long enough, is usually fatal to a relationship. While a specific level of soul compatibility is preexisting between two people, it is the subconscious record of each person that can limit and hinder the level of soul compatibility that each couple is uniquely capable of achieving.

Subconscious records are the conditioned and habitual ways, tendencies, preferences, mannerisms, attitudes, desires, and behavioral characteristics permanently recorded in the subconscious minds of each partner. Subconscious records are developed by a lifetime of everything you've ever experienced, every second you've lived—and no two people have the same subconscious record. Over time, the subconscious records of any two people naturally will begin to bump up against each other, contrast, and conflict with each other. How these conflicts are resolved determines the status of every relationship, and, unfortunately, in many cases, the status of the relationship determines the status of a person's life.

The subconscious record of a person is more deeply recorded in the mind than even most scientists of the subject realize. The question, then, is: when these deeply rooted differences between people inevitably clash, what is to be done? Which partner relinquishes their preferences to accommodate the other, and consequently remains dissatisfied, unhappy, and frustrated because of the sacrifice? And how often do these concessions by one partner or the other occur, to what degree, and in how many different areas?

For average people, satisfying their preferences, desires, habits, and material goals determines the quality of life. For above-average people, discovering and fulfilling their true purpose determines the quality of life. When an average person relinquishes their preferences, desires, and ways, there is a significant feeling of disappointment with little compensation. When an above-average person sacrifices their preferences and changes their ways to accommodate their partner, they move a step closer to soul compatibility. When average people sacrifice their habitual preferences to accommodate a partner, they achieve, in a sense, a moratorium of natural discord and improve their traditional existence. When above-average people change their ways and habits to create harmony in a relationship, they are allowing the contents of their souls to connect and interact.

The key for above-average people is to always focus on the goal. Whenever a partner's ways, habits, preferences, reactions, or moods are challenged by disharmony within a relationship, the partner who must make the change should not focus on what must be forfeited by the change, but what can be gained by the change. Above-average people must rise above the level of their subconsciously recorded preferences and their characteristic behaviors, which almost always relate to a person's comforts, entertainments, sensual wants, moods, ego enhancements, and the tendencies to establish the familiarities of one's past.

Remember, it is a person's subconscious record which always interferes with soul compatibility.

For each partner to sacrifice certain preferences, change certain habitual tendencies and reactions, and discipline certain moods which interfere with the harmony of the relationship is to achieve the potential for soul compatibility. Satisfying one's own preferences, desires, and ways without changing one's self results in living at the same level of life for an entire lifetime. Achieving soul compatibility with another person achieves a dimension of experience that far exceeds a life of continually attempting to satisfy personal preferences and material goals, regardless of how successful their endeavors may seem.

When an above-average person becomes aware by communication or observation that there is something about themselves that should be changed to improve the harmony of their relationship, then it becomes vital to the grander scale of the future that a change be made—and this applies equally to both partners. This understanding should be established.

Averageness at its best is still averageness. The goal of above-average people in relationships is to achieve the potential of soul compatibility unique to each couple by removing the obstacles sourced in the subconscious records of each partner in order to achieve something which few people ever understand or experience.

One could mistake this information as standard advice for improving a relationship, but there is nothing commonplace about removing the obstacles for soul compatibility—i.e., creating the conditions and cooperation for the contents of two souls to work together to achieve an innate potential.

Most people rely on careers, hobbies, travel, entertainment, social activities, ego enhancements, advancing their material positions, and traditionalism in every form to get satisfaction from life because they do not achieve the degree of soul compatibility with another person that makes life extraordinary—the extraordinariness experienced when two people are in a relationship and, at the same time, are helping each other achieve their true purpose in life. Beyond all that is traditional, for above-average people, this is the purpose of a relationship.

True Love

Once, during an office visit, a patient told his doctor, "This is the worst pain I've ever had." The doctor said, "Every pain is the worst pain you've ever had."

For most people, love is something like that—in the positive sense. Each time they fall in love, they feel they have met the true love of their life. But seldom, if ever, does anyone maintain the emotional high a person usually experiences when they meet someone new and fall in love. The rapture resulting from a new love wears off over time and becomes something less enthralling and less all-consuming. Most of the time, from what at first feels like your supreme love, a commonplace relationship develops, or the original feeling of love changes into dislike and separation results.

True love can only exist when you have found the right person. The right person is the person who naturally creates the necessary emotional environment for you to discover and fulfill your true purpose in life.

Unlike other emotions, which are more easily defined, love may be one of the most difficult emotions to describe because, while each person uses the same word "love," the scientific feeling of love is different for each person, as each person is different from one another. While dissecting love scientifically is hardly romantic, for the above-average person, the information is worth knowing.

Love is not one emotion or human connection. Love, unlike hate, envy, and empathy, is a complex combination of instincts, varied feelings, and habit patterns. Most feelings of love are sourced in the subconscious mind and are generated from a person's subconscious record, i.e., conditioned by each person's unique lifelong record of every experience they've ever had. Almost all feelings of love are unique combinations of personality attraction, need, security, dependency, a survival instinct, familiarity by association and subconscious record-matching, possessiveness, maternal instincts from women, protective instincts in men, and even circumstances. No two people have the same combination of factors that determines their feelings of love. No two feelings of love are exactly the same, and every person's experiential definition of love is uniquely different from everyone else's. Everyone in the world may use the word "love," but everyone is referring to their own unique feeling and referencing love by their own unique standard and capacity.

To understand the nature of love, one must understand that the differences in human beings are far more than physical differences, personality differences, intellectual differences, and the differences developed by upbringing and a person's environment. One should understand that, as a factor of nature, with regard to human beings, an evolutionary scale exists, and that human beings are born at different levels on the evolutionary scale.

Every person's concept of love, reference of love, and feelings of love, are based on their evolutionary status. The less evolved a person is, the less is their capacity to give and receive love. The more evolved a person is, the greater their capacity to give and receive love. Technically, love itself has a scale, and each person's love exists at a different point on that scale. People experience love at many different degrees of intensity, and people feel love for each other for a combination of many different reasons. Many partners may remain together for life, and over time, many partners may develop strong attachments to one another, but none of these forms or degrees of love may be considered true love. True love results only when there is a mingling of soul content between two people which serves each one fulfilling the true purpose of their life. Needless to say, true love is rare! It has a dimension that all other forms and degrees of love do not have.

While true love is difficult to describe, because everyone interprets it by their own experience, standard, and capacity, there are certain manifestations in a relationship where true love exists. These are some examples:

While partners in all relationships experience some degree of accommodation and sacrifice to maintain the relationship, true love generates feelings of freedom and relief for each partner, much more than it does feelings of responsibility and sacrifice. Whether a person realizes the full degree or not, because the precise measurement is relegated to the subconscious mind, most relationships eventually create a greater degree of feelings of restriction and psychological weight than they generate feelings of freedom. Most long-term relationships create a desire for freedom and a constant subconscious seeking of freedom, even within the context of appreciating the benefits of the relationship, and even when certain forms of love may exist. While true love is scientifically and cosmically mysterious, and somewhat inexplicable, it can be measured. If a long-term relationship feels restrictive, often smothering, and "weighted," i.e., antagonistic to the feeling of freedom, even if there exists some form and degree of love, *it is absent of true love*. Experiencing a feeling of freedom and relief from the weight of life when you are with your partner is one of the defining characteristics of a relationship where true love is present. If being with your partner feels like the path to freedom and to achieving true purpose, that is a sign that true love exists in the relationship.

True love creates a psychological environment that encourages each partner to pursue their true purpose. In most relationships, one partner is usually more materistically inclined than the other, and consequently, is always attempting to force on their partner activities and involvements of their own preferential and desirous lifestyle. Where true love exists, neither partner will constantly pressure the other to participate in the type or amount of activities their partner would not choose if they were not in that relationship. Where true love exists, one partner does not feel they are always being pressured to accommodate the preferences, needs, desires, lifestyle, and timing of the other. When an above-average person is in a relationship where they feel a constant pressure—verbally or vibrationally—to accommodate their partner, it is usually not a relationship where true love exists. Time is a very precious and irrecoverable commodity; overly accommodating the demands, desires, and needs of a less sensitive and more materialistic partner is usually time lost in pursuit of one's own unique purpose.

True love creates an atmosphere where a person feels comfortable being completely open and honest with their partner. In most relationships, one or both partners (usually one far more than the other) is constantly forced to be "creative" with the truth in order to maintain peace and harmony within the relationship. In most relationships, the more sensitive or evolved partner does not feel they can be completely free to be themselves and is usually more subconsciously at ease with a best friend or even a stranger. In a relationship absent of true love, one partner usually feels restricted—not necessarily physically restricted, but discouraged from expressing their true feelings, which, even if occasionally expressed, are usually met with an inappropriate response, and consequently become suppressed and submerged. In most relationships, the more evolved and sensitive partner develops a position of being guarded, which in time becomes a subconscious habit pattern. This guarded position eventually becomes second nature and, after a while, is "accepted" as the normal status of the relationship. While a certain degree of love within a relationship may exist, a guarded posture of mind is a symbol of the absence of true love. A person can speak freely and remain completely at ease with their partner when they feel they will not be criticized, misunderstood, ridiculed, or unduly analyzed—verbally or otherwise. In an atmosphere of true love, there is virtually never an attempt at superiority by one partner to demote the intelligence of the other partner. In an atmosphere of true love, a person can be honest because their honesty carries no "penalty." The appreciation of a partner is so high, that the acceptance level is equally high. In a relationship where true love exists, a person feels free to be their true self to a degree they could not be in any other relationship.

True love creates a feeling of constant buoying. True love becomes a force that is constantly uplifting, countering the weight of life that everyone experiences to one degree or another. While every relationship requires some degree of effort and sacrifice, relationships where true love is present require little to no management, compared to most traditional relationships that require a degree of constant management and effort that adds to the difficulties, responsibilities, and the "weight" of life. People in most commonplace relationships know only too well the feeling of tedium and sameness, that no matter how much is done or changed environmentally, the feeling of sameness from the relationships remains ever present—which becomes subconsciously depressive. In almost all long-standing relationships, the partners relive each day within fixed boundaries of experience. For average people, the fixed boundaries of experience are acceptable, even desirable, if the experience and activities are suitable to their nature. For above-average people, fixed boundaries become psychological prisons or lifetraps created by the cosmic limitations of a partner. While no relationship can maintain the artificial high that existed at its beginning, in a relationship where true love exists, there are always positive surprises, a consistent feeling of newness and stimulation, and a powerful sense of gratitude to be with a partner. Where true love exists, there is always a subliminal sense of excitement, instead of (as in most relationships) a subliminal sense of sameness. Where true love exists, a relationship becomes the source of constant restoration and renewal.

A relationship where true love exists creates a state of authentic permanency because the relationship is based on soul compatibility. Most relationships are subconsciously based because they do not have soul compatibility and are, in actuality, states of perpetual temporariness, which many people equate to permanency. Almost all long-standing relationships — even those where traditional forms and varying degrees of love have developed — are actually day-to-day truces, compromises, and in many cases, a subconscious acceptance of the eternal struggle between two people of different natures and different levels of sensitivity. In truth, most long-standing relationships are actually subconscious "contracts" between two people to achieve and experience all the commonplace and traditional activities and goals of life—family, career, companionship, security, material expansion, entertainments, hobbies, and for some partners, even the doing of good deeds—but not necessarily true love or true purpose. Many relationships may become permanent in structure, and certain degrees and forms of love may develop, but in the subconscious minds of most partners, there is clearly registered the feeling of incompleteness and unfullfilment because true love and true purpose are absent in their lives. A relationship that creates an atmosphere in which each partner can achieve their soul purpose is a very different relationship than relationships that serve all the ordinary, commonplace, traditional, and materialistic purposes of life.

While above-average people are especially human, and hardly fail to appreciate other people who are charming, attractive, sensual, talented, intelligent, and interesting, seriously considering having an intimate relationship with anyone beyond their own relationship is virtually nonexistent. In a relationship where true love exists, it is not a discipline, moral obligation, or fear of consequences that keep people from extra affairs, but the knowledge that they cannot achieve with another person—regardless of that person's qualities or attributes—the unique experience they receive from being with their partner.

True love is indeed rare, but it is worth becoming a force whereby you attract true love into your life. Above-average people can become that force.

Until He or She Arrives: Mastering the Art of Living

℘erhaps the greatest misconception about relationships is that if a person does not find the true love of their life, then their life will be incomplete and unfulfilled.

It is true that above-average people are innately and instinctively programmed to seek the "perfect" mate, who, through a relationship, will help them establish the base of comfort and companionship from which they can discover and accomplish the true purpose for their life.

But the reality is: a person can be quite happy and relatively content until their true love appears because Nature is not so unrelenting that it does not offer us alternatives and options, since there are many circumstances and reasons which can affect connecting with the true love of one's life.

You may not meet the right person until you are in your 40s, 50s, or 60s. When you do meet, you or they may be married to someone else, or may be separated by other circumstances. You may have met the person early in life and lost them because you had not yet developed the sensitivity, maturity, and psychological skills to maintain the relationship. The right person may die and be irreplaceable. You may not have connected with the true love of your life because your activities and the busyness of your life obscured your sensitivity and, before meeting your true love, you committed yourself to living with or marrying a person who may be an adequate mate, but definitely is not the true love of your life. Or you may, as many people do, have a series of relationships, affairs, and/or marriages, but ultimately wind up without your true love.

In all of the above circumstances, in the absence of being with the true love of one's life, above-average people are capable of mastering the art of living, i.e., the ability to get everything they need, not from one person, but from a variety of people and a variety of sources to become relatively satisfied and content with life—while at the same time, never giving up the possibility that their true love may appear.

Of course, everyone, in the absence of finding their true love, will attempt (some more successfully than others) to get as much satisfaction and fulfillment as possible from all the opportunities in their environment.

It is an instinctive approach of human beings to extract as much satisfaction as possible from all that exists in their environment, but it is an entirely different approach to master the art of living, which begins by dispensing with the notion that a person must live an unhappy, incomplete, lonely, or unfulfilled life until they connect with the true love of their life—a feeling that exists to some degree in everyone's subconscious mind. It is an aspect of Nature that human beings are programmed to seek their most compatible mate—and the impulse is a strong one, so strong that people very often choose the wrong partner in order to satisfy this impulse.

But once an above-average person accepts the fact they can achieve a state of fulfillment and completion in the absence of finding the true love of their life, then an innate mechanism of the subconscious mind will engage and a natural, high level, intuitive, and creative process will begin to guide you. You will begin to select the people, places, events, and activities in your environment (whatever that environment may be) that will eventually add up to the equivalent, or near equivalent, of having found the true love of your life in terms of the feeling of completion and fulfillment.

Technically, one factor that distinguishes above-average people from average people is that the subconscious minds of above-average people can master the art of living in almost any environment, regardless of its conditions or seeming limitations.

The magic here is: given the lack of opportunities and the seeming limitations in any environment, the choices and decisions one makes may not themselves *directly* provide satisfaction and fulfillment, but what they lead to will bring fulfillment. So, it is not necessarily the person you choose to spend time with who is a piece of your fulfillment puzzle, but the person they introduce you to, or whom you inadvertently meet through them. And it may not be the specific place you decide to go to, or the activity you choose that adds to your feeling of completeness, but, once there, the clues, hints, guidance, and contacts you find that direct you elsewhere to what will eventually result in satisfaction and fulfillment.

In the absence of finding your one true love, you can collect three, five, eight, or more people in a close circle of friends and intimates, and each person provides an aspect of the interactions, stimulation, companionship, sensuality, and even love a person needs to feel satisfied and complete. But this is not a feat that is easily accomplished; it requires the finesse, intuition, and charisma of the above-average mentality.

In mastering the art of living, your subconscious guidance system will select an array of people and cultural, recreational, spiritual, and purpose-oriented sources to create a combination in which the total of its parts equals, or nearly equals, the feeling of contentment and satisfaction that you would experience when the true love of your life appears. And if Nature has its way, he, she, or it will appear at some point in your life ("it" because for some people, their true love is not necessarily a specific person, but a true purpose for their life). This is not to say we should not have both, because it is exactly what Nature intended for us—both the person and the purpose.

But for whatever reason or for however long, until we find the true love of our life, above-average people should rely on the perfect mathematics of the Creation, which determines the perfect balance of Nature. We should consequently realize that, regardless of the circumstances, seeming limitations, or lack of opportunities in any environment, we can cleverly and intuitively manage, combine, and parlay all that is available to us to equal the sum total of everything we need to feel a sense of satisfaction and completion until the true love of our life appears.

What determines mastering the art of living is the ability to get a component of everything we need from a variety of people, activities, and other sources, and make them add up to a complete and fulfilling life—and above-average people innately possess this ability.

True love comes in many forms and from many sources. For some of us, it is finding one other person who is perfectly suited to our nature and our purpose in life. For others, for whatever time-frame, true love can exist in combination, from a variety of special people and a variety of sources. For above-average people, the goal is to master the art of living in whatever form it takes.

Time and Insight

*I*n most circumstances, time works for you when you act quickly—seize the moment, capitalize on an idea.

With relationships, it's just the opposite. Time usually works against you when you commit to a permanent arrangement too quickly, situationally or emotionally.

Emotions always obscure insight, and the more a person is gifted with insight, the more their insight is obscured by emotionalism—the type of emotionalism that usually accompanies a new or relatively new relationship.

Above-average people should understand that while a person's personality is to a large extent the result of upbringing, conditioning, life's experiences, and innate degree of sensitivity, almost everyone's personality has been ingeniously crafted by their subconscious mind to disguise the deeply rooted, habitual defects in a person's nature—the kind of defects that, when discovered, create distance and disappointment, and can cause termination of a relationship.

One of the many functions of the subconscious mind is that, with or without a person's conscious direction, the subconscious mind takes note of one's own character and personality deficiencies and then, over time, stylizes the personality to cover them up with a deceptive facade. But, as is the case with human ability, some people are innately more skillful than others at disguising their true nature.

It is beyond wise to remain in any relationship at a relatively casual distance until you see the true nature of a person beneath their personality. Or, if your insight is operative at its sharpest level because you discipline your emotions whenever you begin a relationship, you will recognize, to the extent they exist, the deeply rooted habitual defects in another person before you invest yourself too deeply in the relationship.